Strategic Dreaming: Business

Michele Clapp

Published by Ilara, LLC, 2023.

STRATEGIC DREAMING: BUSINESS

First edition. April 4, 2023.

Written by Michele Clapp.

Table of Contents

Table of Contents

This is dedicated to all the entrepreneurs working to bring their ideas to life and share their unique vision with the world.

Here's to making your dreams a reality!

Welcome

Welcome to Strategic Dreaming!

The Strategic Dreaming process combines analysis, strategy, and goal setting. The purpose is to create a tailored blueprint for your business dreams.

This process focuses on solo entrepreneurs, independent contractors, and small business owners to explore their goals, analyze their current business, and create action steps that move them closer to their goals.

The strategic dreaming process is a four-step process. Step one, you will create a vision of where you want to be in a year. Step two, you will explore the present by analyzing different areas of your business. Step three, you will set goals that build a bridge between where you are and where you want to be. Step four, you will map out your goals on a calendar.

Throughout the guide, I provide activities and questions. You are welcome to use those most helpful for you and your business. I also encourage you to answer any questions you think of as you explore your unique business.

How to use the guide:

Chapter sections walk you through the strategic dreaming process. These sections include activities, questions, notes, and holistic notes.

- Activity – prompts to get you thinking and writing about the topic.
- Questions – assist you in exploring different aspects of yourself and your business.
- Notes – prompts to review your notes, add information important to you, and document unanswered questions.
- Holistic Notes – prompts for your thoughts, feelings, and insights.

Some tips as you move through this process.

- Complete at a pace that is best for you.
- Take breaks when needed – I encourage you to take them frequently.
- Be open to the gems that come from taking a step back.
- Take notes as you go.
- Be specific.
- Ask yourself lots of questions.
- Tailor this to suit you and your business – add, remove, and adjust what you need.

Pre-Work

Activity

Before you begin this process, I want you to write down who is in your support system.

Your support network can serve as a sounding board and provide a much-needed break from the analysis.

Questions

Who will you discuss this process with?
Will you discuss this with colleagues, peers, friends, or family?
Do you have a coach you can discuss any questions you have?
Do you have a mentor who can support you through the process?
Do you have a therapist who can support you through the process?
What other resources do you have available to support you through the process?
Each of these individuals or resources has strengths you can use to your advantage. Some resources may be more helpful than others when you have a specific question.

As you look at your support network, what are the strengths of each one?

What else comes to mind for you and your business?

Notes

Review your notes.

What do you notice?

What are you learning about yourself and your business?

What questions do you have?

Keep your support network list handy, so you can reach out when you need support. These support resources can be helpful for any unanswered questions you have.

Ilara, LLC provides strategic accountability groups, coaching, and free resources for small business owners. Learn more at www.ilara.org[1].

---

1. http://www.ilara.org

Step 1: Vision

Activity

In this exercise, you will look forward one year to imagine where you want to be and the possibilities in your business.

Imagine this time next year in your business. Write down what comes to mind.

_____

Questions

What does your business look like?
What are you doing?
Who are you working with?
If you see yourself as comfortable in your business, what does that mean for you (is it financial, environmental, who you work with, etc.)?
How much money are you earning?
What type of work are you doing (specific products, programs, services)?
Who are your customers?
Do you have a team that you are working with?
Where are you working?

What else comes to mind as you look forward?

Notes

Review your notes.

What do you notice?
What are you learning about yourself and your business?
What questions do you have?

Activity

Review your vision.

Be sure it is specific. A detailed description will help you create targeted goals that move you exactly where you want to be in your business.

Activity

Congratulations on crafting your business vision!

Take a moment to celebrate your accomplishment. It is a big deal to create your vision!

Activity

Let's take a deeper dive into you as the business owner. Seeing your vision can be exciting and stressful at the same time.

I encourage you to write down your thoughts and feelings as you encounter them. Your holistic notes can help identify patterns, stories that influence your decisions, and what might be getting in your way. The goal is to use these insights to make positive changes as you grow your business.

Questions

What do you notice as you review your vision?
What thoughts surface for you?
Which thoughts are part of an old story created in your life?
For example, I'm not (fill in the blank) enough to start my own business or be successful.
Where do these thoughts come from?
What can you tell yourself to overcome these thoughts?
How does it feel to see your vision in front of you?
Where do you notice these feelings (head, throat, heart, gut, etc.)?

What are these feelings telling you?
How can you use your feelings to help you make the best choices for you and your business?
What resources do you have to help me navigate this process?
What resources do you need to help me navigate this process?
What else comes to mind for you and your business?

Holistic Notes

Review your notes.

What additional thoughts, feelings, and insights come up for you?
What do you notice?
What are you learning about yourself and your business?
What questions do you have?

Activity

Review your business vision and imagine being there.

Questions

Write down answers to these questions and any others that come up for you.

What do you notice?
What thoughts come up for you?
What feelings come up for you?
What are you experiencing?
What about your vision puts a smile on your face or brings you joy?
What else comes to mind for you and your business?

Notes

Review your notes.

What do you notice?
What are you learning about yourself and your business?
What questions do you have?

You can temporarily set your vision aside. You will use it again in Step 3: Building a Bridge.

Step 2: Present

Now you will begin exploring the current state of your business.

This step allows you to assess what you do, what you have in place, what will support your vision, and what needs to be adjusted.

Take breaks as you need them! This process can require a lot of work to examine the details of your business. I do not recommend doing everything in one sitting. Sometimes walking away will bring areas of your business to light that you had not already considered.

Activity

Let's begin exploring where you are now.

The areas of your business you will explore include:

- Type of Work You Do
- Clients/Customers
- Financial (Income/Sales)
- People (Your Team)

- Environment (Office)
- Operations (Organization, Order)
- Communication (Internal/External)
- Resources
- Competitive Advantage

Do these categories reflect your business?

If so, great!
If not, adjust them to fit you and your business.
Do you need to rename categories, add categories, or delete categories?

Now that you have the categories that reflect your business, you will explore the details of your business. Be specific with each area of your business.

The questions provided are a guide and can be modified to suit your business needs. Use the questions as a starting point to carefully consider your business. As you go through each section, ask and answer questions that come to mind.

Let's get started!

Type of Work You Do

Questions

Tailor the following questions to suit your business needs.

What do you currently offer (services, programs, or products)?
How are you doing in each type of work you offer?
Are you doing well or struggling (services, programs, or products)?
Are customers making purchases (services, programs, or products)?
What are your customers responding to (services, programs, or products)?
Which are your most/least popular (services, programs, or products)?
What feedback do customers give you (services, programs, or products)?
What else comes to mind for you and your business?

Notes

Review your notes.

What do you notice?
What are you learning about yourself and your business?
What questions do you have?

Holistic Notes

Review your holistic notes.

What additional thoughts, feelings, and insights come up for you?
What do you notice?
What are you learning about yourself and your business?
What questions do you have?

Clients/Customers

Questions

Tailor the following questions to suit your business needs.

How many clients do you have?

Who are your clients (the type of client)?

Consider different aspects of your clients (the reason they do business with you, gender, occupation, location, etc.).

Are your current clients who you want to be working with?

How do your clients align with your current business goals?

How is it going with your clients (do you build relationships with them, and do they return)?

What is the typical length of the relationship (one-time purchase, short-term, long-term)?

Is the duration of your business relationship what you want it to be? Do you want a shorter/ longer relationship?

What else comes to mind for you and your business?

Notes

Review your notes.

What do you notice?
What are you learning about yourself and your business?
What questions do you have?

Holistic Notes

Review your holistic notes.

What additional thoughts, feelings, and insights come up for you?
What do you notice?
What are you learning about yourself and your business?
What questions do you have?

Financial (Income/Sales)

Questions

Tailor the following questions to suit your business needs.

How much do you have invested in the business?

How much are you currently earning in your business (monthly/yearly)?

Where is your income coming from (services, programs, products)?

How much are your expenses (monthly/yearly)?

What are you spending your money on (operations, marketing, licenses, education, etc.).?

What are the most/least costly items in your business?

How much profit are you earning (monthly/yearly)?

Has there been a cadence/pattern in the past year?

Do you notice there is a busy time of year or a quiet time of the year?

Do you have a budget?

Do you follow your budget?

How are you budgeting your business money?

How are you at managing what is coming in, what is going out, and deciding the best way to use your money?

What expenses are unavoidable (you can't change them, you must have them to operate)?

Do you have expenses that could be scaled back or eliminated?

How will you scale your business expenses as you grow (based on monthly income, number of customers, etc.)?

What else comes to mind for you and your business?

Notes

Review your notes.

What do you notice?

What are you learning about yourself and your business?

What questions do you have?

Holistic Notes

Review your holistic notes.

What additional thoughts, feelings, and insights come up for you?

What do you notice?

What are you learning about yourself and your business?

What questions do you have?

People (Your Team)

Questions

Tailor the following questions to suit your business needs.

Who are the stakeholders in your business (partners, investors)?
How many people are on your team (employees, contractors)?
Does the number of people on your team meet your business needs?
Is your team aligned with your business goals?
What work do you delegate to your team?
Who do you delegate your work to?
Do you notice a trend of delegating work to a specific team member?
What type of support do you offer your team?
What resources do you offer/provide your team?
What type of development do you offer (training, onboarding, etc.)?
How are you motivating and inspiring your team (do you celebrate their success)?
How do you reinforce what is good and working?
What else comes to mind for you and your business?

Notes

Review your notes.

What do you notice?
What are you learning about yourself and your business?
What questions do you have?

Holistic Notes

Review your holistic notes.

What additional thoughts, feelings, and insights come up for you?
What do you notice?
What are you learning about yourself and your business?
What questions do you have?

Environment

Questions

Tailor the following questions to suit your business needs.

Where do you work (at home/an office)?
Does your environment meet your needs?
Are you comfortable in your work environment?
What equipment do you have to help you get business done?
Is your equipment in good working condition?
What furniture do you have for your business?
Is the work environment working for you?
Is the work environment working for your customers?
How do clients respond to your environment?
Does your environment help you get work done?
What are the advantages of your business location?
What are the disadvantages of your business location?
What else comes to mind for you and your business?

Notes

Review your notes.

What do you notice?
What are you learning about yourself and your business?
What questions do you have?

Holistic Notes

Review your holistic notes.

What additional thoughts, feelings, and insights come up for you?
What do you notice?
What are you learning about yourself and your business?
What questions do you have?

Operations

Questions

Tailor the following questions to suit your business needs.

How do you get your work done/what are your processes (to-do list, apps, etc.)?

How effective are you at completing daily/weekly business tasks?

What tools do you use (scheduling calendars, apps, customer management, email, website, sales tracking, inventory management, etc.)?

Which tools are most effective for you?

What makes these tools effective for you?

Which tools are least effective in your business?

Why are these tools the least effective?

How do you manage your time (scheduling, work-life balance)?

Is your time management working for your business?

Is your time management working for your personal life (allowing balance)?

What times of day work best for you to get your work done (type of work/tasks)?

Have you noticed that some tasks work better for you at certain times of the day?

How are you with making plans and following them?

Who else do you work with as part of your business (vendors, advisors, mentors, accountants, etc.)?

How do these individuals/businesses serve your business goals?
What else comes to mind for you and your business?

Notes

Review your notes.

What do you notice?
What are you learning about yourself and your business?
What questions do you have?

Holistic Notes

Review your holistic notes.

What additional thoughts, feelings, and insights come up for you?
What do you notice?
What are you learning about yourself and your business?
What questions do you have?

Communication

Questions

Tailor the following questions to suit your business needs.

What tools do you use for communication (website, email, social media, etc.)?

How is communication with customers handled?

How do customers learn about new services, programs, or products?

How do you communicate new policies to customers?

What do you communicate to existing customers?

How often do you communicate with existing customers?

How do customers provide feedback about services, programs, or products?

How is communication used to attract new customers (marketing)?

What types of communication do you use to attract new customers?

What do you communicate to potential customers (do you notice a trend to share specific types of information)?

Has your communication been effective in attracting new customers?

How is communication within your business (between and to your team)?

What type of information do you communicate with your team?

How often do you communicate with your team?
Is this working for everyone on your team?
How do you communicate with individuals/businesses outside of your business (accountant, lawyer, vendors, etc.)?
What else comes to mind for you and your business?

Notes

Review your notes.

What do you notice?
What are you learning about yourself and your business?
What questions do you have?

Holistic Notes

Review your holistic notes.

What additional thoughts, feelings, and insights come up for you?
What do you notice?
What are you learning about yourself and your business?
What questions do you have?

Resources

Questions

Tailor the following questions to suit your business needs.

What resources do you have to assist you in business (people, systems, tools, etc.)?
What resources do you find most helpful?
What resources do you have to assist your customers?
How do you use resources to help your customers?
Which resources do your customers find most helpful?
Who are your colleagues?
How do your colleagues assist in your business?
Who do you refer to for anything outside of your expertise?
Where do you go for anything outside your expertise?
Where do you go to find answers?
What resources do you have to assist your team?
How do you use resources to support your team?
Which resources does your team find most helpful?
What else comes to mind for you and your business?

Notes

Review your notes.

What do you notice?
What are you learning about yourself and your business?
What questions do you have?

Holistic Notes

Review your holistic notes.

What additional thoughts, feelings, and insights come up for you?
What do you notice?
What are you learning about yourself and your business?
What questions do you have?

Competitive Advantage

Questions

Tailor the following questions to suit your business needs.

What is unique to you and your business?
What unique experiences do you have?
What strengths do you bring?
How do your strengths help you manage your business (the day-to-day)?
What makes you stand out from other businesses?
What does your team say about what is unique to your business?
What do your customers say about what is unique to your business?
What else comes to mind for you and your business?

Notes

Review your notes.

What do you notice?
What are you learning about yourself and your business?
What questions do you have?

Holistic Notes

Review your holistic notes.

What additional thoughts, feelings, and insights come up for you?

What do you notice?

What are you learning about yourself and your business?

What questions do you have?

Other Categories You Created

Questions

Consider what this category represents for your business.

Why did you include it in your analysis?
What is working?
How does it help your business?
What is not working?
What else comes to mind for you and your business?

Notes

Review your notes.

What do you notice?
What are you learning about yourself and your business?
What questions do you have?

Holistic Notes

Review your holistic notes.

What additional thoughts, feelings, and insights come up for you?

What do you notice?

What are you learning about yourself and your business?

What questions do you have?

Activity

Take a moment to think about your overall impressions of your current business.

Questions

What have you noticed about your business today (any a-ha moments, revelations)?
What would you say is good and working?
Can you maintain the things that are good and working?
What aspects of your work fulfill you?
Can you maintain the things that fulfill you?
What isn't working for you, your team, or your customers?
What else comes to mind for you and your business?

Notes

Review your notes.

What do you notice?
What are you learning about yourself and your business?
What questions do you have?

Holistic Notes

Review your notes.

What additional thoughts, feelings, and insights come up for you?
What do you notice?
What are you learning about yourself and your business?
What questions do you have?

Great work on completing your business analysis!

Take a moment to enjoy the hard work you have done.

I know it can be an extensive and exhausting process. It can also be an exhilarating and inspiring one.
You are ahead of many business owners out there by completing this process.

Bonus Activity

This bonus activity allows you to explore your current level of satisfaction with each area of your business. You can take a step back and get an overall picture of your business.

You can use this information to get an overall picture of your business, identify areas of your business you wish to focus on, areas of your business you want to be intentional about, and use the information to set goals.

Instructions:

Step 1 - There are nine categories to use. You can use them as they are or revise them to represent areas of your business that are important to you.

Step 2 - You have completed an analysis of your business. Carefully consider what each category means to you.

Step 3 - Ask yourself how fulfilled/satisfied you are with each area on a scale of 1-10 (1 means completely dissatisfied; 10 means completely satisfied). A score of 10 does not necessarily mean that the area does not need attention, just that you are satisfied with this area of your business.

Step 4 - Write down a rating for each area.

Step 5 - Review your ratings and consider what it means for you in your business (do you notice any trends, what aspects are you satisfied with or not satisfied with, and how does this align with your analysis). Your ratings can help you decide where to focus your efforts.

Satisfaction Ratings
1 = Completely Dissatisfied/Not Fulfilled
5 = Satisfied/Moderately Fulfilled
10 = Completely Satisfied/Fulfilled

- Type of Work You Do
- Clients/Customers
- Financial (Income/Sales)
- People (Your Team)
- Environment (Office)
- Operations (Organization, Order)
- Communication (Internal/External)
- Resources
- Competitive Advantage

Notes

Review your notes.

What do you notice?
What are you learning about yourself and your business?
What questions do you have?

Holistic Notes

Review your notes.

What additional thoughts, feelings, and insights come up for you?
What do you notice?
What are you learning about yourself and your business?
What questions do you have?

Step 3: Building a Bridge

You will use your vision and analysis to create goals that bridge the gap between the two.

Prompts provide a guide to help you develop goals that move you toward your vision. Some prompts are intentionally similar to help you think of different perspectives. Use the prompts that are most helpful for you and adjust them to suit your business needs.

I encourage you to review all areas to see how each can influence your overall business. You may be surprised to find areas of your business have overlapping goals or some support goals in other areas.

While I encourage you to review each category, some areas of your business will take up more of your focus. That is okay! You will use your expertise and insight to determine where you will focus and how you will work towards your goals.

Tips to consider:

- Be prepared to make tentative goals that you adjust as you continue exploring the possibilities of what you can achieve in the next year.
- Make sure your goals are specific, achievable, and realistic.
- You want to set yourself up for success in a way that allows you to stairstep toward your vision.
- Even tiny steps are steps forward.
- The tiniest adjustment can make a big difference.

Areas of Your Business

You will use the same activity, questions, notes reflection, and holistic notes reflection provided to build a bridge for each area of your business.

Once you complete your bridge work in a category, make note of it to track your progress.

- Type of Work You Do
- Clients/Customers
- Financial (Income/Sales)
- People (Your Team)
- Environment (Office)
- Operations (Organization, Order)
- Communication (Internal/External)
- Resources
- Competitive Advantage
- Other Categories You Created

Activity

Review your Step 1: Vision and Step 2: Present business analysis for this category.

Compare the similarities and differences between the two.

Write goals that will help move you closer to your vision.

Questions

Have you achieved your vision in this area of your business?
If not, what steps can you take to make your vision a reality?
Does this area of your business currently support your vision?
If this area supports your vision, how can you use it for your overall business or for other areas of your business?
If this area does not support your vision, what needs to be adjusted to move in that direction?
How can you adjust this to achieve your vision (put something in place)?
What do you notice as you review your holistic notes for this category (any revelations)?
How can you use your holistic notes to help you in your business?
What would you need to have in place for a positive holistic experience?
What do you need to support yourself more holistically?

What other steps/goals come to mind as you work through this process?

What resources/skills do you have to help you achieve these changes?

What do you need to help you achieve these changes?

What obstacles are holding you back (will keep you from achieving your goal)?

What can you put in place to help you overcome that obstacle?

Review all of your goals in this category.

Can your goals be broken down into smaller goals?

Are your goals specific?

Does the goal address one item or multiple items?

If multiple items, break them down into smaller and more specific goals.

Is the goal achievable?

If not, consider how to make adjustments that move you closer to your vision.

How will you track your success with this goal?

How will you recognize/reward yourself for achieving this goal?

Notes

Review your goals.

What do you notice?

What are you learning about yourself and your business?

What questions do you have?

Holistic Notes

Review your holistic notes.

What additional thoughts, feelings, and insights come up for you?
What do you notice?
What are you learning about yourself and your business?
What questions do you have?

Step 4: Mapping

Now you will map out your goals on a calendar to help you take steps toward your vision.

You may discover that some goals overlap, some must come before others, or there are too many for the month.

Go ahead and adjust your timetable to make it manageable.

Your goal is to make progress each month while keeping it realistic.

Activity

First, determine how far out you want to plan. Will it be for the next year, the next six months, or the next three months?

Three months is a typical timeframe to work with so that you can come back, evaluate, and make adjustments as needed.

Create a calendar based on the timeframe you selected.

Activity

Determine how you want to approach this process. There are different strategies for mapping out your goals, depending on what is most helpful:

- Work on goals for all categories
- Select what is most important to you
- Select what you can achieve quickly to launch you into bigger goals
- Select the biggest challenge for you

There is no right or wrong answer! Consider what is more likely to motivate you and keep you moving forward.

Activity

Determine how much time you have available to focus on your goals.

Evaluate what is already on your calendar (business and personal).

Areas of Your Business

You will use the same activity and questions to map your calendar for each area of your business.

You can map goals from all categories or focus on the categories that are most important to you.

Once you complete your mapping work in a category, make note of it to track your progress.

- Type of Work You Do
- Clients/Customers
- Financial (Income/Sales)
- People (Your Team)
- Environment (Office)
- Operations (Organization, Order)
- Communication (Internal/External)
- Resources
- Competitive Advantage
- Other Categories You Created

Activity

Refer to the steps/goals you created in your Step 3: Building a Bridge work.

Select a goal in this category that you want to focus on in the next several months.

Place the goal(s) on your calendar.

Select the next goal and place it on your calendar.

Adjust your goals as needed. It is typical to make adjustments as you map out your goals to make sure they are manageable.

Questions

When do you want to have this goal completed?
How much time will it take to complete this goal?
Does this goal need to be completed before another goal?
Does this goal need to come after another goal?
Will this goal be challenging (meaning you might need more time)?
How many goals do you have in the same month (too many or time for more)?
Do you need to adjust your goals based on business or personal events (due to your available time that month)?

Wrap Up

Congratulations!

It can be challenging to move towards your business goals and dreams. It is also a worthwhile process.

Remember, you can adjust your vision and goals as you grow, learn, and take steps forward. With your Step 1: Vision and Step 2: Present analysis in hand, you can explore what to adjust. When you need, return to sections of this guide to make adjustments as you continue to move toward your vision.

I encourage you to set a date in three to six months when you will check in on your strategic dream. You may discover slight changes to your vision, needed adjustments, pitfalls to address, and what is right on track.

Keep up the great work of going after your dreams!

Check-in

This section provides some guidance on doing regular check-ins of your strategic dream.

I encourage you to do this every three to six months. You may discover slight changes to your vision, needed adjustments, pitfalls to address, and what is right on track.

Use the questions provided to analyze what is right on track and what can be adjusted, added, or removed from your plan.

Activity

There are different methods you can use to do a check-in. I provide some options below for you to consider (or come up with one that is perfect for you).

Consider the best option for you.

Options for completing the check-in:

- Go through the four strategic dreaming steps (your previous work will make this a quicker process than the

first time you walked through the steps)
- Focus on specific areas of your business
- Use your prior strategic dreaming analysis to create the next three to six months of goals (continuing to work on goals you previously identified)
- Use the prompts provided below
- Use a combination of these options based on your insight and expertise

---

Questions

Were you able to complete the goals you mapped out?

If you completed your goals, take a moment to celebrate your success.

What has helped you complete your goals?

How can you maintain what is working?

What has been challenging about completing your goals?

What got in the way of completing your goals?

What changes can you make to address these challenges?

Did the goals need to be broken down into smaller parts?

Did you need more/less time for each goal?

What resources do you need/have to help you overcome these challenges?

Reviewing your vision, is this where you want to be in the future?

If your vision has changed, what needs to be adjusted to represent where you want to be in the future?

Reviewing your present analysis, does this reflect your business?

If not, what needs to be adjusted to represent your business today?

What do you notice as you review your holistic notes?

How can you use your holistic notes to help you in your business?

What would you need to have in place for a positive holistic experience?

What do you need to support yourself more holistically?

What other steps/goals come to mind as you work through this process?

Create a calendar based on the timeframe selected (3, 6, or 12 months). A three-month calendar is provided at the end of this chapter – after Holistic Notes.

Select a goal from your building a bridge work.

Decide where to place the goal on your calendar (based on the time to complete it, if it comes before or after another goal).

Evaluate each month to see if your goals are manageable with your business and personal events.

Notes

Review your notes.

What do you notice?
What are you learning about yourself and your business?
What questions do you have?

Holistic Notes

Review your notes.

What additional thoughts, feelings, and insights come up for you?
What do you notice?
What are you learning about yourself and your business?
What questions do you have?

Acknowledgments

First, I have to thank my mother. You supported me throughout this process and gave your feedback on the design of the cover and the interior (again, and again, and again).

To my peer coaches, Austeja, Brittni, Lynn, and LaPora, who have supported me and this project in a variety of ways; Austeja for giving me space to talk about the concept and helping me own it, participating in a live session, reviewing a draft, and providing valuable feedback; Brittni for listening, supporting, and always believing in me, for reviewing a draft of strategic dreaming, and for providing insight and feedback; Lynn for participating in a live session and sharing your perspective; and LaPora for reviewing a draft of this project and giving your feedback.

To my dear friend, Ayanna, you came into my life when things were their craziest. You supported me wholeheartedly. You listened to me share my dreams, believing in the possibilities before I did.

To all the entrepreneurs, leaders, and individuals I have coached, who have participated in Strategic Dreaming, and who shared what has or has not worked for them, I am honored to work with you and to learn from you.

Credits

Cover photography by Michele Clapp.

Also by this author

Strategic Dreaming: Journal
Strategic Dreaming: Weekly Planner
Find the most updated list at: https://www.ilara.org/books

About the Author

Michele Clapp is a personal and professional success coach working with individuals charting a path toward their dreams. She works with individuals to identify their current reality and explore options that make the most sense for them. Greater satisfaction, peace, productivity, and success is the goal. Michele owns Ilara, LLC, where she supports individuals on their journey toward their dreams. Michele has a Ph.D. in Psychology, specializing in psychology in the workplace. She has worked with individuals and organizations across the U.S. and internationally. Additionally, she holds several coaching certifications, including being a Board Certified Coach and a Whole Person Certified Professional Coach. If you would like to explore other books by Michele Clapp and what is coming soon, go to www.ilara.org/books.

Read more at https://www.ilara.org.

About the Publisher

Ilara, LLC provides personal and professional success coaching.

We work with individuals to discover, create, and walk a path that is true to where you are today and where you want to be. This is an opportunity to explore those areas of your professional and personal life most important to you, to develop and implement strategies to reach your goals, and to make adjustments that maximize your effectiveness.

Our approach is supportive, empathic, and collaborative. We use powerful questions, active listening, reflections, exploration of your options, and action planning to propel you forward. We will collaboratively explore, create, and walk a path forward that makes the most sense for you.